Octave Shifts for the Cello

book one

by Cassia Harvey

CHP104

©2004 by C. Harvey Publications All Rights Reserved.

www.charveypublications.com - print books
www.learnstrings.com - PDF downloadable books
www.harveystringarrangements.com - chamber music

Octave Shifts for the Cello

book one

Practice Suggestions

1. Connect the lower notes with the higher notes. Keep your finger on the string as you shift.

2. Shift at an even speed, with clear notes before and after each shift.

3. Shift with the finger you are going to. Midway through the shift, the fingers should come together on the string. The new finger takes over from the old finger.

4. Play with full bows and strong tone.

5. Use vibrato as much as possible.

Octave Shifts for the Cello

Book One

Cassia Harvey

I

©2004 C. Harvey Publications All Rights Reserved.

Octave Shifts for the Cello, Book One

2

©2004 C. Harvey Publications All Rights Reserved.

3

4

5

6

7

8

9

10

11

12

13

14

15

16

17

18

19

20

21

22

23

Octave Shifts for the Cello, Book One

24

©2004 C. Harvey Publications All Rights Reserved.

25

26

27

28

29

30